Pet Grief
How to Cope Before and After

Jackie Weaver
'The Animal Psychic'

Other books by the author:
Animal Insight
Animal Talking Tales
Celebrity Pet Talking
The Voice of Spirit Animals
Animal Communication from Heaven and Earth
For the Love of Pets
Real Animal Communication Stories No.7

**Psychic
Book
Press.com**

ISBN 978-1727127782

1st November 2018

I dedicate this book to Sally, the Angel on the cover, who truly was sent from Heaven to

help and heal.

To all the amazing people and animals whose knowledge have helped me to write this book,

I thank you.

Through suffering, wisdom can come and light can shine brightly once again.

DEALING WITH THE DEATH OF YOUR PET #ThisMorning

ITV This Morning September 2016

I was delighted to help edit yet another book for Jackie, although this one is a different type from her Animal Communication ones. Speaking from personal experience and as 'guardian' to many pets over the last few years, I take from this book a wonderful lesson in self-help at times of great stress, anxiety and grief. I tell my dog every day how much I love him and how special he is to me. In return, he gives me more love and affection than I could ever know. I know that the sad day will inevitably come which is going to be one of the hardest I will have to endure, however, the lessons that Jackie sets out in this book are invaluable and something that I will, and have, taken on board for future reference.

Shirley – Author. North Wales.

Some years ago, I met Jackie when she was a speaker at an International Animal Conference. We instantly struck up a friendship as we are alike in many ways. We also share a common aim in life, that is helping others and bring happiness where we can. Jackie, like most people, has had to overcome many challenges in her life. Her job comes with many pressures and responsibilities, especially when under the media spotlight. It has been a privilege to demonstrate the techniques within my work as an emotional and behavioural specialist to help conquer unwanted emotions, design, and enhance her life so she can be strong, cope with adversity and continue helping people and their animals in the pure and beautiful way that is Jackie.

I am so delighted to read in this book, Jackie sharing how she has utilised these processes and techniques aiming to give you choices which can to help you through the grief of your pets. It is beautifully written, clear, practical, down-to-earth and easy to understand. Jackie has a huge and genuine heart. She truly wishes to empower you with strength and knowledge so that you can cope through your pet grief, before and emotionally heal after. Let us not suffer more than we need to – I am sure our pets who have passed on would not want us to.

Maureen Fearon – Emotional and Behavioural Expert. Manchester

My Darling Stan 2010 - 2013

Introduction

I am truly honoured to do the work that I do. Even if you are not into the spiritual side of life – pet loss hurts us all just the same. In life, I am actually a very logical, generally down-to-earth person, but also have emotional journeys to deal with too. I too have experienced that desperate, and all-consuming pain, of losing a beloved pet or cherished animal.

Through my animal communication work, people contact me who are often experiencing heartache and loss. My aim here is to help you 'before and after'. We all know that one day their life will end and dread that inevitable day. This book is not about animal communication, unlike my others but through my work, I have learnt and been shown so much, so I hope at least some of this imparted wisdom will help you, as it has many others.

Over the years, I have helped people in many different ways, before their animal has passed and after too. As in life, when managing 'human' situations, mind preparation can really help give us strength and clarity when we need it most.

From my work, animals do understand what you say. Whether you believe that or not, it is immaterial to understanding the help I hope this book offers you. If you doubt it, just take one minute and imagine what would it be like if it was really true? You could say what you wanted and it would sink into their minds, so why not just say all that you want to anyway. You have nothing to lose and they have much to gain.

My intention is to cover as many facets of the grieving process as possible and hope that it will help ease your pain. Also, and very importantly, to try and help banish those inevitable mind games that we, as people, put ourselves through: Will they forgive me? Was it the right time? Did I do enough? Am I to blame? Did they suffer? Did they have quality of life? What if I get another pet? Etc. Etc.

As I write this, I truly am experiencing the 'before' grief stage. Sally, my angel on Earth, may still be here whilst you read this, or have passed to spirit to meet up with my other pets that have gone before. And, not only pets, people too. At this time, Sally is rising 14 years old and suffered two strokes within the last 6 months. Amazingly, she has rallied round and shown such strength of character. This is from a dog that had such a terribly abusive start in life and was rescued by a social worker. Basically, the social worker saw this terrified seven-month-old pup and after a few hours of persuasion, she managed to take her away with her. What a lady, and for that I will always remember her. The next day, I was at the vets at the same time and said how lovely she was. Her response... 'She needs a home!'

I was very very ill with cancer when I got Sally but felt it was all meant to be. She was my focus and my husband's constant companion throughout that time. It was Sally who told another communicator that I too could communicate with animals. She has brought so very much to my life and is a teacher for everyone too. Even now, she is sharing lessons here! I adore her.

My life has been far from straightforward and if I ever write an autobiography, you will be pretty surprised at the things that I have had to overcome, complete with the many funny happenings too I might add. I am one of these people who somehow manages to see the funny side in not the best situations.

One of my life tips I will share with you now… Think to yourself, what are the type of stories we tend share at a later date? They usually are of when things went wrong! So, my way of thinking (as long as it is not something sad, debilitating etc.) when a situation happens for example: you bump the car, fall over and ruin your outfit on a special occasion, bump into an ex in an awkward situation, the list would be endless of life's mishaps. At that time, I say to myself, 'One day I will laugh about this!' It really does help and then I get on and deal with whatever happens. So, maybe try that yourself? You have nothing to lose and maybe ease your mind in a situation.

Back to my Angel on Earth, Sally. Well, I say mine, you may be surprised to learn that she actually lives with my ex-husband, Bob, and has done the past couple of years. We split up and eventually got divorced. I bet your gut reaction is, 'Why did you not take her with you?' Well, talk about sacrifice…

Sally, then aged over ten, had lived with us in the middle of the countryside and become a confident girl in her own way. She also had her two cat companions too, which she follows about and checks on. She thinks she is a nanny! (She previously had our darling cat Stan, whom she was besotted with. He sadly died on the road, aged three and a half. I will talk about him later.)

I however, moved to a very busy, non-countrified place. I had brought her here for a week as we intended to try and share her as best possible. I realised that she was worried as there were so many dogs and people which she was not used to. She had gone from a hamlet of 24 houses to my town consisting of 10,000 people!

She was not her usual relaxed self, apart from with me in the house. So out of love, I let her go back to all that she knew and was comfortable with. I am lucky to be on great terms with Bob and I still see her. She looks after him and the cats, and that is her place in life. She helps me with my work and has taught so many people how to communicate with animals, so has been an inspiration for many.

Did the decision break my heart, yes it absolutely did. I felt like I was grieving as no longer could hug, kiss, walk and be able to physically show love to the dog I had shared ten years of my life with. With help from friends and seeing her as happy as she was, I knew it was the way it was supposed to be.

I wish back then I had known some extra techniques to help manage my mind. Our thoughts and feelings are very complex but also 'trainable'. We form habits easily, so we can also train our minds to help us with 'good thinking' beneficial habits too.

An example of how our minds are 'genius'. When you go to brush your teeth in the morning, can you recall exactly how, and in which order, you do it? I bet not. This is because we have done it that many times, our sub-conscious kicks in and guides us. It is like when you are driving; once you have learnt how to do it, got used to it, you can easily have a conversation at the same time. This is because your genius mind goes on to a sort of 'auto-pilot' to let you do both. Even further than that... How many times have you driven a few miles and realised that you cannot totally recall doing it? Our genius brains just 'do it' on a kind of auto pilot but should anything unexpected happen, our clever mind kicks in and gets us to brake or do whatever is required. I can feel the nod of your heads. Only joking, but I bet you are.

So, imagine if we could use this thought process to alter our minds to try and help us? The good news is... We can!

The conscious mind is doing all the day to day work, like a computer. Sometimes it would be better if a program was changed or sent into the background (sub-conscious) or even better, sent to the TRASH! If something in your computer is not serving it well, then you would try and get it fixed. Guess what? Our brains work in a very similar way. Life happens – things can go wrong and 'infect' thus causing other running programs to go wrong too.

On a computer we can send things to trash however, as you know, somehow that lovely little computer chip can actually still hold that information. This is why in life, something that can seem small can overwhelm us. This is because our fabulously clever subconscious is like that computer that is holding on to everything regardless, and then matches things up with the here and now. It thinks it is helping, however, what it does is cause an overload of upset by bringing up other things just to add on top.

There will be things you will have 'forgotten' (buried in your sub-conscious) not totally cleared that can bounce back up and create even more upset. This is possible to clear and we will come to that in the chapter, *Allowing Yourself to Heal.*

Although this book is written to help with pet grief, you may find you also can apply some of my learnt wisdom to your life. I have been so very fortunate to have been helped to overcome many things and realised my learning can help others with their emotional pain.

Life with our animals is often not straight forward. We do our best and deal with things in all different ways. What binds us all in this book is our absolute love of our animals and trying to do our best for them.

I will guide you through my thoughts and offers of guidance from when: your pets are happy and living with you, to dealing with life when they are maybe not so happy, to making the decision, and when they have passed over. When you read 'happy', 'not so happy' – this too can be part of it. Personalities traits / attitudes / way of being can change, just as it can do in people. This is when our minds really can get scrambled and unnecessary guilt can creep in.

However, animals are amazing and have an incredible and straightforward view on things.

Even when animals are going to Heaven, they are so accepting and understand that this is out of love and care. It is us that have the doubts and heart-wrenching pain. So from my experiences, I hope to help you through the grief journey… I do not write this saying it will not hurt. Oh yes, it will. There is nothing we can do to avoid that. You have just lost someone you truly and utterly loved with every sense of your being. We are human so it is a natural and a totally understandable emotion. However, my aim is to help you get through it the best way that you can.

Before we even start, I want to share this simple, yet amazing technique, that can help so much when you are in a stress / panic / emotional situation.

Some of you may know of EFT (Emotional Freedom Techniques) where we tap on certain points of the body to stimulate a response. Even if you don't, you can still use this. There is science behind how the process works, but for now I am keeping it in the terms of my own experience. I am not an EFT teacher although my amazing friend Maureen Fearon is. She's an emotional and behavioural expert. She has taught me, and helped me, so much. So from her, to me, to you...

On this diagram, the spot highlighted at the centre of the chest is over the Thymus Gland. (It is so very important, yet never really mentioned. Well worth a quick look on the internet.)

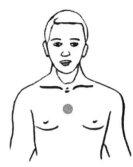

So, when in a situation that you have an unwanted heightened emotion, with your hand curled towards you, gently tap / drum your fingertips on the point as marked. At the same time, take a deep breath, then release the breath all the way out whilst looking upwards. You may wonder why the direction you look in affects you. Well, you know that saying, 'looking into the depths of despair', when sad / troubled etc., it is what we do. I am sure you will have noticed, that when people are feeling down, they do tend to look downwards. That clever brain of ours will go building the feelings and thoughts to match. So, do the opposite and simply look up, and your brain will not add to your sad emotions and won't invite the usual patterns that can devastate or make us feel sad etc.

Just keep tapping and breathing. Imagine breathing those feelings or thoughts out of your body as you do not want this painful feeling inside. You will probably notice your breathing slowing down as you start to feel calmer. You will find that although the situation is still the same, you are feeling calmer and more in control without the added emotions that are not helping you.

This is great if you feel like you are on the brink of crying and at that point, crying is really not what you want to do.

(Crying can be useful to us: it is a natural way to release emotional pain. So, if you feel the need and it is not going to affect what you are doing, let the tears flow. We all know, from previous times, they do eventually stop. This is about having choice with our tears. There are times, and places, where we just do not want to cry.)

I love this saying, '*Tears are the words the heart cannot say.*'

Practice this tapping technique (for your reference, it is actually known as Inner Re-Patterning) for even small things that you have to cope with, as well as grief. I have used it that many times, it is second nature to me now. If you can picture this… I was doing a slot on TV – *ITV Loose Women*. They asked me to give info on two of their animals, which escalated to four, then at the last minute, rose to five. All this to be done in a seven-minute slot! Some challenge as you can imagine. Apart from giving the info about each of their animals, I had to be calm enough to deliver it clearly and be ready to be 'questioned / judged / doubted' – which I definitely was! However, having tapped and tapped beforehand, I held my own and actually managed to achieve what I wanted and gave animal communication credibility.

Seriously, give it a try – you will see.

*****

Living for the Day

When you truly love your pet, sometimes we cannot help but think of that terrible, terrible day that will inevitably come. This is because we love them so very deeply irrelevant of their size and breed. From horses to hamsters they can be like our children to us: sometimes in a mother to childlike bond or simply as we adore them and do so much for them – just as we do for a child. I hear people saying to me that they feel so terrible as they feel even more upset about their pet passing than when a parent did, this to me is totally understandable, although not to everyone.

With people, we do not tend to worry so much as people are designed (although this is not always what happens) to have a longer length of life. This being the way it is, would not be such a logical thing to keep reminding ourselves that this time will come to an end? Do we really keep doing that? I don't tend to think so. Whereas with our animals... We tend to have an age expectation in our minds which is 'normal' but not a useful thing to dwell on.

Some animals live a shorter life, just due to their breed. Others really amaze people and reach 'unexpected' ages. Our minds use the 'normal' and 'unexpected' to form thoughts, feelings and sometimes grief before they have even completed their lives!

During your treasured animal's life, when, although they seem fit and healthy, how many times have you said, 'I have no idea how I will cope when they have gone?' 'I will never get over it', 'I love them and can't bear the thought'? At that point, you may be feeling part of a grieving process that has not even come your way! Maybe it is time instead to think, 'I need to bear the thought.' Ask your clever and helpful mind, 'What is the best, and happiest way to feel, at this time?' It should give you a good instruction that is *best* for you. Think of it like this... What would you suggest to a child? Ever heard of the 'inner child'? It simply means, if in doubt, think of yourself as your child and what would you suggest to that child?! Sounds simple, and do you know what? It is! Again, this can be used not just for the grief process, but life.

I have to say – I totally understand those 'end of life' thoughts that want to keep popping up. Having an animal that is so precious, who gives you unconditional love, and accepts the same from you, no wonder you would dread all of that ever ending. However, the inevitable is the inevitable, as it is in people. So isn't it a good idea to help yourself and do all that you can, when you can and still have the time to do so. At least you can do your best to avoid that, 'Oh, I wish I had done this, and wish I had done that!'

*****

Making Memories Whilst You Can

As in life, we know that things sometimes don't always go to plan. However, live your life with them, as if it should do so. (I know due to ailments etc., sometimes it is not so possible.) We humans sometimes like to make a 'bucket list', as we like to call it. So why not think about all the things that you would like to look back on, and make the memories whilst you can.

This does not have to entail serious, important things, simple things can be just as good. I remember making the effort to go to a local show with my dog. I am not into showing at all, but it was a day out and he won the best rescue! It warms my heart to see the picture of that day and I know how much it meant to him.

Animals are not judgmental and if you picture a place you would really want to take them, then put it on your list and do! Imagine looking back regarding your dog and saying, 'Oh I wish he had had the chance to go and meet my lovely friend and her dogs. He would have loved that.' If you have the chance, make that memory.

If you have a horse, not all horses are fantastic competition horses – some are just amazing companions and easy riding horses. So, think of what is suitable for them and for you, and maybe try it. If it is not an action thing, maybe find a friend to take a video of you doing 'your thing' or set up a photo session, professional or otherwise.

The one thing we all hear people saying, 'If only I had taken a picture or video of them doing that.' My darling cat Stan who sadly lost his life on the road, used to stand up on his hind legs and kiss me on the lips when I asked. Do I have a video of him doing it? No, and gosh how I wish I did. I had plenty of opportunities but, for whatever reason, I thought, 'I must do that sometime.' Suddenly at three and a half, he was gone.

My thought process for you here is… spare five minutes to sit down and think of all the wonderful/cute/funny/clever things your pet does and if you would you like to have that memory to treasure?

Yes, you have it in your mind, but if you can, and want to have it in another form, do it whilst you can. Put it on your bucket list and make the time. It may only take minutes but it will give you something to treasure forever.

*****

Quality of Life

This is such an emotional turmoil in our heads and hearts. We love our animals and do not wish them to suffer. We seek veterinary advice and do what we feel is the best for them. Sometimes it is not as clear cut on a medical level, so here are some thoughts for you.

So often, when our pets are elderly, they lose mobility and their movement is curtailed. There are many conventional and alternative treatments to help with joint conditions. No animal should suffer pain, just like you would not want a human to. However, as I often point out, even if your granny cannot run up the street like she used to, is she still happy/adapted to a more sedate life? People adapt and get used to people looking after them instead and accept (sometimes begrudgingly) that age comes to us all.

We do not put people down just because they can not do what they used to, so… look at the quality of life your animal has. Animals are great at listing things to me when the quality of life question is asked. (I have a lovely video of a chat with a very elderly cat telling his owner, his point of view. It is on my You-Tube channel. He really did state his case and was still happy.) I think the best marker is – are they doing most of the normal things still? Are they still: loving towards you, still interacting, still eating enough to keep going comfortably in themselves? (Regarding weight, yes an animal in senior years can gradually lose weight. This again can happen to 'granny' but as long as they are happy, it is a normal process. Sudden weight loss should obviously be investigated by your vet.)

A real tricky one is, if your animal has, for example, kidney failure. I have to say I really dislike the term 'failure'. It instils immediate fear in our hearts as it sounds final. My choice of words would be kidney problems / kidney issues / degeneration of the kidneys. If you have say, arthritis in your knees, it is degeneration. They do not say you have 'knee failure' – it just means that you have an aged part of your body that needs help to function as best as possible.

Back to the tricky issue… Often your vet will suggest that they can no longer have their usual food and no treats etc. Some pets cope, others just point blank refuse their change of food and are sad because they no longer can have treats. I cannot suggest you go against your vet's advice however, if your animal is really miserable and not eating, this may not be beneficial to their declining health either.

Once again, your thought process is to weigh up their present quality of life. If you really did have to give them what they are willing to eat, then surely that is better than them being ill due to not eating or feeling thoroughly miserable in the late stages of their life? Sometimes you can cheat and mix, and as for treats – often they are happy because you are simply giving them a treat. So, maybe you could get away with giving them very small portions of the treat, so at least you are still giving.

Sometimes, you have to judge what is more important, especially if they are aged and have another illness.

Here is something one of my animal communication clients has written for me to share with you:

My cat Tinkerbell who at 14-years-old has an on-going illness relating to her mouth and having treatment for that. However, after one of her blood tests, I was told that her kidneys were starting to show very low grade degeneration. She is old, a very fussy eater with an incurable mouth issue and is on steroids and pain killers for it.

I was in a dilemma: do I try to change her to bland veterinary food as suggested due to her ageing kidneys when I know that she will not like it and choose to starve. Believe me, it has been difficult enough throughout her life to keep her interested in food. I love her dearly and want the best way to help her but most of all, her to be happy.

When Jackie asked Tinkerbell for her thoughts, she pointed out that at least she was still eating in spite of her mouth problems, and showing no obvious issues with her kidneys. (Had she not had a blood test, Lisa would have been none the wiser.) As for Tinkerbell's mouth issue, it is a very serious one that sadly is getting worse, so, if possible, to keep things the same as they are. However, should she start to show kidneys symptoms, i.e. noticeably drinking more, then time to reconsider.

We are now six months on and she is still with me, eating her favorite foods, showing no kidney issues, sleeping a lot, but content with it. I know that her time is limited but glad that she is having things the way she wanted and why not? As a person, if I had an incurable condition, I would hope to still be able to eat what I wanted if that was the least of my problems.

Lisa O'Donnell – Watford

People often say how worried they are as their pet is now sleeping so much. Again, people that are aged do the same – it is nature. As long as your pet is able to do usual things like; eat, toilet, interact in some way and are not showing any signs of serious discomfort, then is that nature's way of them slowing right down in their late phase of life.

*****

Practical Mental Preparation

We all hear those adverts on TV about 'making arrangements' for 'that' time. As with anything in life, you actually do get used to it and when we hear them, they do not cause us pain or panic – they are the 'norm'. They are actually about cost and people's thoughts about organising things to save stress at a future time.

We do not need to do anything here like the adverts do, so no free pens on offer for you! However, on a serious note, take the time now to sit down and think about when that time comes, what would you want to happen? In the midst of that awful time (expected or unexpected), your mind will be in an emotional state.

My great friend Maureen also taught me that logic and emotion do not function together – and it is so true!

A great way of looking at this is to use the Emotion versus Logic see-saw.

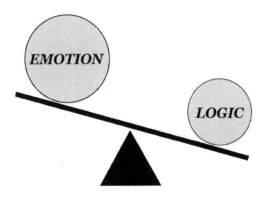

So, when we are in an emotional state, logic really is out of balance and is not helping us make the best decision possible at that time. I recognise this and have learnt to step back, take a deep breath, totally breathe out, and ask myself,

'What is the most intelligent thing I can do at this time?'

This is such a useful practice to learn for life. Perhaps write it on a piece of paper and try to learn it and then use it – you will be amazed how it can help. How often have you fired off that text or email and thought afterwards, 'I really wish I had not done that.'

This just gives your mind the chance to pause and your brain to think and suggest the 'most intelligent' thing to do. You are basically instructing it to work in the best way for you.

Your mind will take instructions, don't we do it all the time? Yes, we do! For a simple example, you say to yourself, 'I must go to the shop and get some milk.' Your mind will take that instruction on board. You will buy your milk with ease and not a lot of thought. (Occasionally we will forget, but we are human, not perfect!) To have the word 'intelligent' in there, also instructs your mind to find the most 'intelligent' solution too!

You can try to use this practice in an emotional turmoil regarding your animal, or during a human situation. You pause, breathe, and flick the question to yourself and maybe find your action the better, and a more sensible one.

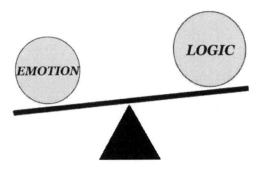

Whatever, there will still be emotion there, be it anger, love, frustration, the list is endless of what we have to deal with and endure. However, if you are in a more controlled mode, your logic is able to work to help you.

Here is a cracking line I love…

'Confusion comes before clarity.'

It is so true. How many times have you had things go round and round in your head? Eventually, as with everything, there is an outcome that will appear through that fog. So, when your mind is whirring, remember that it is a process and, like at every other time, in the end (however long it takes) there will be a result, which gives us clarity. It may be a good or bad result, but it is a result and an end to that whirring and confused mind.

I digressed there but knowing that has helped me so many times, I felt it was useful to share. Anyone who knows me, knows that I can talk for England and when I teach Animal Communication, I go with the flow and fit the points in as I go along.

So... we now know that our brains can get used to most things, the posh word being, 'desensitised'. Just think, if you go back awhile in time and you saw a totally bald man (or woman) your mind would instantly wonder if they had got cancer, alopecia or suchlike. Roll on to now, it is the norm for men to completely shave their heads. So, we have got used to it and do not even notice it as different – our brains have accepted it as 'normal' or 'usual'. Desensitising works by the repetitive process. The more you see it, do it, hear it, the less you react to it. (Obviously I am not talking here about traumatic situations etc.)

At this point of your animal's life, whilst they are fit and well... you know what is inevitably going to happen at some point. However, having done some thought planning now, this will allow you to cope better with the emotional situation of losing your animal. You will not have the added stress of trying to work out extra things, as you have 'pre-planned' and know the answers already. This way, you can concentrate on what you need to and have less added confusion and worry, and even regrets.

I have written you a list and if you have a family, you could maybe ask them for their input too. They may find this a little difficult so maybe an apt time is just after one of those adverts has been on, and then have a general conversation. In happy and non-stressful times, this will be a hundred times easier than when dealing with your grief / their grief at the same time as losing your pet.

A similar way of thinking is when you are going abroad on holiday. Isn't it great when you have your case packed, passport, tickets, insurance and everything done? Isn't that a great feeling? You can then relax and get on with your holiday. However, if you leave it all to the last minute (I bet some of you do) then maybe a hitch will happen. This can cause you to be anxious, even panic, and that is just a holiday – not you losing / loss of your beloved pet. Get the info for whatever your preferred choices are and just put it away for whenever you may need it:

- List of names and numbers of all who need to need to know straight away.

- Would you keep some hair/mane? (You can do it now and put it away.)

- Put to Sleep – at the surgery or at home? If at home, where would be suitable for you and the vet?

- What would you wrap them in?

- Would you want a toy / collar etc. on them, or would you rather keep it?

- Would you like a toy / note / something of yours to be put with them?

- Would members of your family like to see them after they had passed?

- Would you want to show them to your other pets when they had passed?

- Cremation – so find out where that would be? What would be your preferred choice of place and crematorium people?

- Would you want to share or scatter the ashes? If so, to request that the casket / urn is not sealed.

- Burial – where you would choose and is it practical? Would it worry you if you had to move?

- If this is not an emergency situation, how would you really like to spend their last day or night with them? What would you want to do? (I bought fillet steak for one of my dog's last meals – it makes me smile to this day.)

- If you are making a will, think of what you would want for your animals, should anything happen to you.

- I am sure you can add your own important things to this list too.

Another point to perhaps consider… Your pet is very ill and being operated on. The vet then phones you to say that whatever was wrong with them is actually inoperable, and suggests it is best that your pet goes to Heaven. Often it is suggested that they are put to sleep on the operating table so that they never come round. I, as an ex vet nurse, always thought this seemed very fair and sensible.

However, if your animal is seriously not in pain, (you could ask your vet to administer a dose of high strength painkiller) then if your animal was allowed to come round, although they would be very sleepy, this would give you a chance to say goodbye if you wanted to.

Please, if you are reading this, and are thinking 'Why didn't I think of that?' then it wasn't for you at that time. It is only through a reading that this came to light and so I realise that this really could be another option. As long as your animal will not suffer (they shouldn't due to the drugs and anesthesia) this could help ease your pain and suffering of not being able to give them their last kiss and goodbye whilst still living. Again, this is something to consider should that situation ever arise in the future.

*****

Don't be Afraid to Ask or Say

They say, 'knowledge is power' and that is such a true statement. I hope this book will help bring you added peace and the power to achieve that. Most of us are not vets but we do have common sense.

Here is maybe a different way of thinking as I bet you, just like me, have also been in a situation and felt that you really could not speak up or are not being listened to. This also applies to even less important things when your mind is saying, 'This is not right' but your words seem inadequate or you actually stay silent! Your mind thinks, 'Well they are the professional and they would have my pet's best interest at heart?' This may be true, or is it? I work as 'the voice' for so many animals, and therefore I feel it only fair, and with a sense of responsibility, to share these thoughts with you...

Without putting a too finer point on it, years ago you had to be a vet to own a practice. Most of 'the old fashioned' vets seemed to be a vet for the love of animals. Nowadays, vet practices are all becoming large corporations with financial gain in mind and targets! Has a vet ever suggested an operation / treatment for your pet that you have found rather surprising and seemingly unnecessary?

Okay, so let's turn this scenario around. For example, say you have an old parent in a nursing home. Here in the UK we have (at present) the National Health Service so most medical treatment is free. If you are abroad, the bills are paid by insurance (if they agree it is necessary), or by you.

So let's imagine you have a very old relative who is known to have a serious heart condition. They start to show even more heart symptoms: breathing problems, coughing and have fluid accumulating. Doctors inform you that, in spite of all the medications they are on, and the results that the X-ray shows, clearly there is nothing else that can fix their heart. Do you think they would start to offer you an MRI to show you this? After all, the simple X-ray showed exactly what was wrong? Or, would you suggest they do it at your cost, although it would simply show what they already knew? Would it make sense to arrange for your elderly relative to be transported to a hospital (maybe not that close either) to have this done? Have I got you thinking?

So back to your pets... When I was a vet nurse, MRI's were not available to pets. Don't get me wrong. MRIs and such like (I have had plenty) are such a useful invention for situations where nobody can work out what the actual problem is, or need to see exactly what is going on. For that, they are absolutely brilliant and can be life-saving... *life-saving* being the keyword here. If things are really going to be changed i.e. life-saving for 'old parent' or your old beloved pet, then 'Yes' would absolutely be the right call.

We do not want our pets to go through any more than they medically need, and our bank balances lowered in the process. Once they have done the usual things, such as bloods and X-rays for example to give you their diagnosis, we have the right to ask questions. Always remember: They are your pet, you love them more than anyone and you want what is best and fair for them.

So, do a couple of long breaths in and out, think logically (as best possible) and ask something like,

'With what you know and can see (if they had an X-ray/scan), what would you be able to do?' In many cases at end of life, not a lot can be done to really change things. They may be able to have medicines to help with pain etc., for their final weeks, or days. We all come to the end (well on Earth that is.) However, it will give you information and enable the vet to state their opinion and advice.

Don't be afraid to ask questions such as: Will it show anything different? Will you be able to change the outcome? Realistically what are their chances? (Remember the quality of life too.) Ask for time to have a think and maybe discuss with a partner, friend or relative. That way, you can have time to think (use your EFT tap to calm down if needed) and then come to a not-so-rushed decision.

Back to the elderly relative, would the nursing home be offering an MRI or suchlike at this point which is not making them money personally, but at cost to a health system? So for pets, guess who is the paying health system here... YOU!

You know I have mentioned practices offering surprising operations, well here is an example: Recently, a friend of mine who has a healthy, although totally deaf, dog was informed that she should book her in to be spayed – aged twelve! Her dog was not ill and showing no symptoms, and she was at the vets for something minor and totally unrelated. Fortunately, my friend had the strength and knowledge to speak out. She pointed out that unless there was a very good reason, (which there was not) she would not put her dog through such an operation for which there was no need!

Why would she put her dear dog through major surgery especially at her senior age when there are risks and pain involved, for absolutely no reason? She left, most unamused. So be aware, and be informed. As I said, unless your dog is seriously ill and time is not on their side, take the time to check things out for yourself if you have any doubts at all. Remember, we have intuition too, so heed to it!

Don't get me wrong, there are still some vets out there who do have the animal's best interests at heart. They are wonderful and we are so very grateful – but sadly it seems the way of the world that the small independents get swallowed up by the large amalgamations.

Back to the list I talked about putting together earlier before the future sadness arrives. If you have a list completed, you would have an idea of what you think would be right for your animal and sits well with you. Whatever, at least, you have ideas / knowledge lodged in the back of your mind to recall when needed and hopefully be strong enough to ask what is of benefit to your pet, or not.

*****

If that 'Decision' has to be Made

The most common fear anyone has is about having their beloved animal put to sleep. We as humans may try to 'beat ourselves up' mentally, and this really does not help us at all – it does not let us grieve as we naturally should.

In the majority of cases, to utter those words that you wish your animal to be put to sleep, should usually and hopefully, be in calm circumstances. In these cases, it is still exceedingly hard but you are doing it because you love them and cannot bear them to suffer.

However, sometimes you can get offered veterinary treatment that leaves you to choose if you want your pet / animal to have treatment or not. That is huge and again, you are likely to be in the emotional state, and maybe not a very logical one.

At this point in time, whilst your animal is still with you (maybe even once you have read this book) try and decide if you were in a medical situation, what would you think would be the fairest thing to do?

It is my belief that 'we all come in with a day to go out'. In other words, our arriving and leaving date is set. This may sound odd to you, but in life and even situations seemingly desperately unfair, things have been shown to me (and other people) that allow me to have the acceptance of 'what will happen, will.'

I will share my personal story with you, on two accounts.

Back in 2005, I had Non-Hodgkins Lymphoma. I was Stage 4 – which means it had spread far and wide in my body. I actually managed to have two types of it (B. Cell and T. Cell) just to make things even more complicated! I had a large stomach tumour which then gave me secondaries to my liver, spleen, bones and resulted in the specialist giving me four weeks to live! (They only told me this afterwards when I asked if they expect the tumours to leave my liver as quickly as they did.) I had suffered hugely but completely defied the odds and my oncologists were baffled, as were my doctors. For whatever reason, it was not my time. We may think that doctors, the universe, or even our ourselves are totally in charge. I, however, think there is far more to it than this, and life is a journey that we go on, and the outcome is, the outcome.

So, say for example, if your animal needs a duration of intensive chemotherapy, what would you do? I have already done my own thought process for my other dog who is a large Jack Russell terrier: At that point in time, I would research the survival rate, side effects etc. and unless proven very high plus with side effects I felt tolerable for my animal, I would decline.

This is only my opinion: Animals are designed to live far shorter lives than people. Therefore, my logic is that I would rather spare him that kind of treatment and discomfort, if there is no real chance of truly extending his life and having quality with it too. This is not because I do not love him but it is my informed choice. I listen to what comes through my work and what the real statistics at this time are.

In the state of emotion, hearing that your pet has cancer, you may choose for them to have treatment, or may not – out of emotion, your choice may have been different.

Yet, if sadly he was in an accident and needed one of his legs amputated, I would have it done. My informed choice is that I know he is a fairly light dog and would cope well if he was fit and well enough to deal with it. So, by having passed these thoughts through my mind now, I would be able to answer with clarity even if I was in an emotional state.

When you have a quiet moment, try and ask yourself and others that need to be involved too. Sometimes people can be divided. So, it is much better to come to a point of agreement now if possible, rather than in the midst of a crisis.

Please also remember, you have the say in any circumstances. The veterinary profession is there to give you their informed advice but the animal is yours and the final say should be yours! I only write this as, sadly some people feel so very guilty because they felt 'rail-roaded' into treatments that they wish they had had time to think about. This then added even more pain to the grieving situation that they found themselves in.

Unless it is an imminent life or death situation, be brave and say that you need time to think. They should respect your wishes and if they are not doing so, then would you think they are being fair to you and your animal? Perhaps think of them like a doctor and your child – you have a say. They are *yours* and you know them better than anyone. This way, again, you will be able to make your own decision about what you believe is right for you, and most importantly the pet you love.

Sadly, if your animal is to be put to sleep, your heart will feel like it has been smashed into a thousand pieces – I know, I have been there many times. It is such a terrible thing to deal with. People find it very hard to cope, even knowing that it came from the love of their animal. You will not be letting them down, it will be their time and how it was meant to be.

I work connecting with spirit animals and they gave me this poem... It is to try and help people realise that what they have asked to be done, was for all the right reasons and to never blame themselves. Animals know that you love them and only let them go because it was right to do so.

Letting Go

Your heart is bursting, searing with pain
That physical touch never to be had again
You only let them go because you so clearly care
They might not be here but they are surely up there.

You feel the pull and the tear of your heart
You feel torn inside and ripped apart
The enormity of choosing what best to do
It was done with your love, as they looked to you.

We don't enter into this without thought or care
We do it because the compassion is there
The choice to stop pain and distress of the one we love
Can only be guided by you and the angels above.

Many spirits have come through and given me their word
Your tears of sorrow and distress they heard
But they are free and happy and hold no ill will
Whatever was wrong could not have been cured with a pill.

The height of pain is a measuring device
It shows how deeply you felt throughout their life
With your love given for this most selfless act
They at least left this earth with their heart intact.

Now up yonder and free to roam
This is another level, like a new home
The day will come when you go up there too
They're ready and waiting to meet and embrace you.

If you truly did this from your genuine heart
You were so brave and helped them depart
Your love and courage was seen from above
This really was your strongest act of love.

If you could ask them now, what might they say?
'In my life, that was actually only one single day,
Please remember the rest, the joy, love and play,
For I look down from above and remember it that way.'

As time has passed you may at last feel some ease
Maybe a pet has come for you to please
Animals are not selfish and want you to share
They left that space for another needing your love and care.

We are truly honoured to share in their space
Think back and let that smile adorn your face
The precious time you had could never be measured
Your lasting memories are of those you truly treasured.

Jackie Weaver 2009

I hope those words have gone some way to help you and let you know this from the pet's perspective. I loved the line they gave me, '*In my life, that was actually only one single day*' which is so very true. They live on, so passing over really was one day in their life.

*****

Coping with the Unexpected Passing

Shock compounded with losing your pet is just simply unbearable. I know as my cat Stanley got hit and killed by a car – the pain of that memory is etched in my mind forever.

Animals' unexpected pass-overs aren't just from road traffic accidents but in many ways, some worse than others. There is no easy way of dealing with this and you will probably 'beat yourself up' as you go into a numb mode, and that feels wrong too. This is nature trying to help you deal with it, so your brain can comprehend what has happened. It is totally normal – not because you don't care or don't care as much as you think you should. You are just emotionally in such pain that your minds help you in the best way they can at that time.

As with humans, life can throw us such sadness and when we least expect it. Some people experience quite a few and then think, 'Why me?' or, 'It must be me!' It is neither, it is just that animal was designed to have a short life, but their life was to be lived with you.

They do say that we are never given more than we can bear. I am sure many of you reading this will have experienced tragedy and maybe several and never thought you would get over them. Yet, you are still here.

When a passing is unexpected, we think of the 'What ifs' and the, 'If only I' but in reality we would not choose to be careless, ignore what your animal is showing – things happen and the world is full of accidents, unexpected and even unexplained reasons for passing. We as loving people will try and push blame on to ourselves, yet in most cases, it is simply one of those tragic things.

Horse owners will appreciate this… How many times have you gone past a field with all sorts of dangerous objects like, loose wire, scrap metal and terrible fencing, yet those horses never seem to get hurt. Us, well dare there be the tiniest bit of sharp wood, tree branch or stone in the otherwise perfectly managed land and ours will still find a way to hurt themselves. It is just life and the way things are.

To try and help yourself through this and realise that if this is unexpected, then how were you to know? I am psychic and I don't get to know about my own beforehand either. Imagine, because of my work, if I did know an impending fate? Gosh, my life would be full of worry, and unable to change anything as fate is fate.

You know I said that I believe that we come in with a date to go out? Well here is my own personal example of my cat, Stan's passing back in 2013, aged three and a half. (My logical, well self-blaming brain, actually wondered if I had caused his accident by calling him in at that time.)

I will say however, a couple of weeks before Stan got run over, I did have an odd feeling like we were on borrowed time. (You may have had the same sense with your own pet – just a knowing, but not really knowing.) There is nothing you can do – it is just an uncomfortable feeling that you cannot put your finger on.

In 2013 I lived in the middle of the countryside with Bob my ex-husband. Every night, before it was late, I would call Stan to come home. He was not a wanderer but made the most of the farm opposite and the quiet country lanes. Earlier at 6pm he was sat on the patio with his new collar off once again. (He had the same type for years but this new one, he kept getting off. At the time I moaned thinking it must be faulty, although did not seem so.) I spotted it, put it back on and gave him a kiss on his head as I always did at the same time. I said I love you and off he trotted.

Not long before 9pm I called him to come in but he didn't arrive. I, being me, set off to get him as usual so he would be safe in for the night. Within five minutes of our house, I saw him on the road and just knew, he was gone. I ran to him, picked him up and ran home. The tears roll as I write this.

All I could say to Bob that Stan was dead – we were completely, and utterly, numb. It was the longest and saddest night ever. In morning we got up and buried Stan beneath a beautiful red beech tree. I didn't want to hang around home so suggested we went to see my husband's mum who was in her mid-eighties and in hospital.

She was rather confused and heading for dementia. My husband said, 'Sad news mum; Stan got run over last night.' She instantly replied, clear as a bell, 'I told you I dreamt that two weeks ago!'

Shocked at this, I asked him if it was true. He said, 'Yes.' I was quite taken aback and he quickly explained that he did not want to panic me on what his old mum had said. We would not have changed anything – he loved his outdoor life. I am so grateful that he managed to get that collar off again to have that last kiss and love from me. (Needless to say, I am now terribly grateful for the collar being as it was.)

It did not take long for the penny to drop... I realise that spirit very cleverly had chosen my mother-in-law to casually pass information third hand. This instantly resonated with me and bore out the fact that although I wanted to blame myself for calling him – his date had arrived and spirit had cleverly, but gently, let me know in their own way.

I absolutely love my work but sadly do hear of some terrible ways animals have died. Accidents / incidents and more. I am sure, sadly some of you will have experienced this with your pets and struggled to comprehend how they felt, and wished they had not had to suffer.

If this helps... the body can do an amazing thing – it can disconnect (disassociate) the mind from the physical and emotional pain you would associate with that situation. This is also what shock is part of. Shock can make you feel numb, go into a different state of mind – this too happens with animals.

You, I am sure, have heard when someone breaks a leg for example, it actually only hurts when their mind goes back into normality and realises what has happened. Animals are very adept at shutting down in unhappy situations and so in trauma, they can easily disassociate.

So, when an animal has a trauma and then passes over (or goes into an unconscious state) their minds have 'disassociated'. In other words, the mind feels it would be too much to bear so uses this disassociation so the pain or comprehension of what is happening / has happened, is like a blur and not understandable.

From this, as hard as it is, and if you are suffering, please try to think of all the wonderful days they did have and the love you gave them for however little or long time. I will share another technique of how to help you not focus on the last day/days of their life, but their life. Sometimes, especially in trauma situations we are left with that terrible 'unwanted video' or 'sound track' going round in our minds. In the chapter, *Allowing Yourself to Heal* I will give you techniques to help with that too.

Letting Go of Guilt

Guilt is a powerful emotion however, it is one that really does not serve us well, unless you can go back and change what has happened. If indeed you can, that is great. It is worth remembering, you can apologise to your animal if you blamed them for something they did not do. This way you will feel better and so will they. None of us is perfect, we need to remember that.

I always recall when I first learnt that I could communicate with animals; I was so happy and eager I decided to go and have a chat with my horse, Misty. I started to apologise for doing this, and for doing that and after about five things she stopped me by saying, 'We make mistakes too you know!' How true is that? I have never forgotten it and Misty (now living in Heaven since 2007) will be proud to be sharing her wisdom here. All living creatures will make mistakes – it is life! I will take this opportunity to share a funny guilt story from one of my clients. His dog Bonnie in spirit, gave rise to a bit of an injustice...

I have a few dogs. However, when my German Shepherd dog Bonnie went to spirit, I wanted to check that she was okay. She chatted and then showed the opening of a fridge door, some 'counter surfing' and admitted to being a rather greedy girl. I laughed but then suddenly realised that I'd always blamed my other dog Zak! He is another GSD dog with an equally keen eye and appetite. During the reading it dawned on me; after Bonnie's passing this had all stopped! I then knew who the real culprit was, BONNIE, to which she replied 'Guilty as charged!' I did apologise to Zak who, being Zak, was not bothered anyway, previously or now!

Tim – Bristol

Sometimes we do jump to the wrong conclusion and then feel guilty. Guilt does not help, as you cannot turn the clock back but simply think about what you may have learnt from that.

At this point, I don't know where you are emotionally at the moment: Having suffered a bereavement, or know you are due to face one, or are reading this to help with future thinking, Yes the grief will hurt, but having taken the chance to hopefully make some great memories, done some practical mental planning, I now look to helping you with more emotional feelings and thoughts.

Your emotions will, or are, true and burning inside. You may also be suffering guilt for many reasons. Most turn out to be needless and I will address these.

Putting your animal to sleep I have covered, so please let that go. There is nothing to forgive and be proud that you had the strength to help them, and do what will have been the right thing. Just go back to Stan, it really is the way it was supposed to be. (Further on, I will share some stories of animals talked about before they ever came to their owners. More proof that so many things are set out.) Whether by way of an accident, put to sleep, passing naturally when you were there or not, it is all life's ways.

The guilt of feeling worse about this than your own parent's passing. (This tends to be of aged parents who had reasonable length of life.) Yes, many of you will relate to this as I often hear this one. So why would I say, this is absolutely understandable? Because our animals are like our children. They depend on us and we love them like a child.

Our parents going to Heaven is something that we are brought up with as natural due to age and expected to happen at some point. (Our minds are more desensitised to it, as 'normal'.) As we grow and become independent, animals become our dependents. We give them all the love and care we can in our own motherly, or fatherly, way. To lose them is so emotionally hard and compounded by the fact even if they do have a full length of life, it is never long enough.

So, aim to avoid feeling guilty. If your parent has passed, they would want to hug you, to try and ease your pain, not be angry that you are hurting more now than you did when they went. Also, remember circumstances may have been different in your life then too.

I will digress slightly as we are talking about people and animals. Here is another guilt trip we may go on...

Many people manage to complete a 'normal' length of life cycle that often leads them to getting old and grumpy. Take a 'father' for example. In your eyes, as much as you love him, he has become this man who has no tolerance and really lost his sparkle and interest and is no longer acting like the man you once knew. In fact, when you visited, in the end it felt more of a chore as you were not able to love him in the way you wanted, as he could not receive it in the way he used to.

Think of love like this... love is love but works how it is actually received. The more your pet enjoys your love, the more you give and the deeper it goes. Some pets adore affection and how wonderfully our endorphins bounce with joy as we kiss them and shower them with love. The more they want, the more we are able to give and in turn, we receive. Some are not that fussed and have it on their terms and when they want. We still love them, but the ones who reciprocate our love again and again, then inevitably you cannot but help form a stronger loving bond. It is just like people!

Here is an example from another of my communications...

I rescue Cavaliers and have many of them, past and present. I struggled with the guilt of feeling far sadder for the loss of a certain one, more than many of the others.

My mind was eased when my dear little dog explained that we are not in charge of our strength of love - it is the way it is supposed to be. Jackie clarified this by pointing out that, as in the human world too, some we find are absolutely everything you could wish for, and more. This does not take it away from others, but lets us understand not to feel guilty about your loving bond with the 'special one' (or ones) but to rejoice in the fact that you were lucky enough to have / or had them in your life.

Becky – Bliss Cavalier Rescue, Lincs

So, if we go back to your 'father', now grumpy and old, this I believe is nature's way of weaning you off him. So instead of the strong, full of wisdom and strapping man that you once knew, he now no longer is that. Although you have love and feelings still, but they have changed. This is just the natural course; nature's life cycle should we live long enough to achieve it.

People often want to apologise to their pets, talking about how sometimes they are /had been 'short' with them in various situations. For example, when you are tired and for whatever reason, the dog that used to sleep all night, now keeps getting you up for no reason. We are human, and do get tired. That cat that loved to be with you and no longer wants to be picked up and petted, you may question why and feel resentful as you still want to love them. They might have got to the phase of their life, like a person, where they are switching down, and can't be bothered!

It maybe hard to not think about the times we may have been short, unfair etc. but we do the best we can in whatever situation we find ourselves in. Sometimes that animal is no longer behaving like the sweet funny pet you once had and you are trying to adapt too. We are all different, otherwise we would all be able to be fantastic nurses, counsellors etc. We are not, and all our lives are different.

Another kind of self-blaming is when one animal is very sick, so you have devoted your time to it. When they have got better or passed, you feel bad as you did not have enough time for the other animal. Do you know – animals understand way more than your realise and would not want you to feel bad when you were trying to help another and… sometimes time is limited. If you have done the best you can in a situation, then accept that that is the way it was.

If you feel guilty, that won't serve you well or change anything. However, if you now do have the time once again; do what makes you feel good to make up for it. They will enjoy it and appreciate your love and kindness.

*****

Allowing Yourself to Heal

They do say 'hindsight is a great thing' and imagine if we could use it to our advantage NOW?

What if you had the realisation that these feelings *will,* and *do* pass. Yes, it takes time, and this varies from person to person.

However, with some knowledge of how our minds work, we can make, or even shorten, this emotional journey on a less bumpy road than we thought.

There is a wonderful thing called the Change Curve. Another gem I was shown by my friend, Maureen. She helps people with all varieties of problems and whatever the problems are, they will have emotions attached to them. Her world opened my eyes learning about EFT (Emotional Freedom Techniques – using Tapping), NLP (Neuro Linguistic Programming – words and thoughts to retrain our minds) and so much more. These are all designed to help get our brains to do what is best for us, and make life smoother where possible.

Knowledge is so powerful and suffering is terrible in whatever form. Big or small – it still hurts! However, what if it could be less, or at least in a more controlled way? Remember the tapping on the Thymus point I shared with you earlier? Maybe you already have used it. After all, I am sure many of you reading this will be experiencing grief at this very time.

This is my grief version of the Change Curve...

As you see there is a curve and we will work from the left hand side and follow the emotional process. You will recognise it and have experienced it some time or another in all sorts of ways. Just knowing that we can, and do, come out the other side is a huge positive and emotional power for our minds to know.

If you follow the arrows, it really is what we all go through.

- Death will lead us to the pain of grief.

- In time, we go into acceptance.

- Eventually we go into the healing phase.

- Once we have gone through that, we reach happiness and hear ourselves laughing once again.

This is all very natural and the way of life. Now you have looked at it, I am sure you recognise this pattern. Now try this... Think back in time to a terribly sad point in your life that you have gotten over. It may or may not be uncomfortable to do, but do it anyway. Have you done that now? That is a memory, but it does not have that huge, stomach churning, emotion attached to it anymore. Your mind has processed it through the 'grief curve' and it sits in your subconscious (our mind's computer base) as a memory as part of your life. So, however you feel at the point of grief, it does pass, even though at the time you may not believe it will.

What I take from this, I will share with you. Yes, many times I have experienced loss of my animals at various points of my life. The feelings have been, just the worst ever, apart from losing my father when I was 17, which was indescribable at the time. I do like people, but prefer animals; My life has been with animals through and through. I wish I knew back then what I know now – that in time, I will come up the other side, and life will feel happy once again.

You can also apply this to all sorts of things that life throws at us. Life is not always easy and when you look back, gosh, at the time you never thought you would get over it, yet you did. So maybe at this point, without experiencing emotion, force your mind to recall a sad emotional human happening from your past and remember just for a second how you felt. You healed and came back to happiness. We are stronger than we think.

It is like accepting that this is the way life is, and like it always does, it *will* pass. Another emotional issue will come and you start the curve again. Maybe think of it like having a cut... Imagine if you didn't know it healed? How much worse it would be. However, we do know it will heal and, although it is not good at the time, we have the acceptance that it *will* heal. Some cuts are deeper than others yet they do heal, although with varying times. Sometimes we will scar but often, we can't even recall where we were cut or what it was that happened. We have all leant that you cut and then you heal. It is a similar natural process.

One thing that we all suffer from, even if your animal has a gentle passing, is that we tend to focus on the end. (When our pets pass over in terrible ways, road traffic and worse, our minds seem to want to constantly play that awful video in our mind. It is like stuck on replay and so very hurtful, like a bad habit. I will come to a way of shifting that bad memory video secondly.)

We are in a state of emotion and our minds keep bringing up the pictures and thoughts to go with the emotions. This is not helping us, so try instructing your brain to make a different habit.

Say for example, if you had your animal put to sleep. Your mind keeps taking you to those last minutes. I suggest to people that as soon as your mind takes you there, instruct it to give you a happy memory. This might sound difficult to achieve but do it all the same. The next time it tries to take you to the sad time, instruct it again to give you a happy memory. Your mind will soon form the better habit so when it tries to send you to the sad moment, it will divert and produce a happy memory for you. This is you re-training your brain to a good habit to help you look at the positive times, and not the negative. It truly is possible.

Animals are quick to point out that they do not wish their owners to dwell over these sad times but to look at the amount of good times they had. In most cases, their 'end time' is a mini percentage of their life.

Now to help with the traumatic / sad / haunting, that ever repeating video in our mind. Remember, most of us have been here before too and it did eventually pass. However, it can be so painful, often intolerable. It is not of any help to us and stops us on our road to recovery.

We did not choose whatever happened to be as it was, so here is a process to help. Once again, credit goes to my amazing friend Maureen and all those clever people who understand that we really can retrain our brains etc. Their approach has helped others, and with these gems, we too can help ourselves.

The process is to re-direct your mind but in a stronger way than my first suggestion. That 'bad video memory' as we shall call it, keeps on playing. The more it plays, the more it is in your conscious mind and just won't shift. It is a bit of like a song, that keeps getting repeated, in the end you can even recall the words, although consciously you did not set out with the intention to do so. The more your mind thinks about the bad video, the more it will. Along with it, all those emotions will be triggered off once again and any other similar 'buried' feelings your mind feels that would be 'helpful' (not) to connect with it.

There is a NLP technique called the 'Swish Pattern.' This is my version of it and what works for me. We have many things that 'Trigger' our emotions, and in this case, it is starting that bad video memory. 'Trigger' is a great description as our mind joins things up and fires all sorts of thoughts at emotional times of sufferance. Most irrational but we should not beat ourselves up; Emotion is making us feel 'Irrational' –

quite the opposite of 'Logical'. We have learned that one haven't we?!

The way Swishing works is to force your mind to overlay a bad video memory with a good video memory so the sad/bad video gets pushed to the back of your mind (the sub-conscious), instead of keeping it at the forefront. Think of it like a book you used to refer to – then you found another that you preferred as it was easier to dip into. In the end, the first book will get pushed aside and you will not focus on it, or even look for it, as it has now been superseded by one that serves you better.

So, you want to banish that sad video and have a better one? Okay, let's instruct our mind what we would prefer to watch. Good or bad? It is our mind so let's instruct it to show what we prefer and is best for us.

Sit down comfortably and close your eyes as you are going to purposefully think and trigger that bad video memory. That one you don't want, or need. It is the video that is making you cry all the time, stopping you sleeping, filling you with constant anguish and pain – You really really really do NOT wish to keep revisiting that experience, recalling that video. It achieves nothing, and is not letting you heal.

Please note this process may have to be repeated maybe up to, or at least, seven times, although all at the same sitting. You may have to repeat and repeat after all, it is the most used-to-date bad video, so it is like a strong habit you are breaking. The aim is that eventually, you will not recall that old bad video, but play your good happy memory video instead. It will become the most prevalent and what your mind wants to see / show you.

Instruction one: Think of a good and happy memory. Tell your mind, even say out-loud, 'Give me a good memory' and something will come forward. Select a freeze frame picture of the most positive scene, shrink the picture and make it tiny. Call this picture A.

Two: Recall the event, the unwanted bad "video" that has been revisiting you. Immediately, pause it so it becomes a still picture in your mind. Call it Picture B.

Three: Put the tiny picture A (the positive picture) on top and in a bottom corner, so it's a picture in the corner of the bad video picture (B) as in diagram.

Four: On the instruction, your saying "NOW (you may prefer to say it out-loud as really telling your mind!) the small picture A is going to expand and grow over the bad picture B as shown above.

Do it fast (one or two seconds). You can say out loud as you do it

Five: Repeat again several times. NOW, swish instantly expand the happy picture. Each time you repeat it you will be able to do it even faster as you and your 'computer' mind now know what it is all about.

Six: 'Break your state' Change what your mind and body are doing – i.e. stand up, sit down again, look around you, check your watch, etc. just for a couple of seconds.

Seven: Once again, recall the bad video again. What do you feel and see?

If there are remaining unwanted feelings, repeat the Swishing (step *five)*.

As I said, this may need to be done several times. You will be able to test yourself after doing the process to know it is working. Stick with it. This really is worth doing and won't take you that long.

Get up and walk around for a few seconds. Sit back down and then think of that bad video picture B again. What do you now feel / see? You may find that picture B has faded, is now in black and white or that it doesn't come at all. If only your good memory picture A comes instead, that's great, goal achieved, your good happy memory is now at the top of the list.

If you have to keep trying this, that is okay. Everyone is unique, it is complete when you feel better. As your unwanted bad video picture has been top of your mind's playlist – it may take a bit of effort to push it down the ranks. Think of it like breaking a habit that your brain has formed without your permission.

Now repeat and repeat. You WILL get there.

The beauty of this technique is that once you have learnt it, you can use it again as soon as you need to. You can recall that good memory picture A as often as you like. Each time allowing the positive emotions it can bring.

And, this is not just for your pet grief, this is for all sorts of memories that we would rather forget and knock off our play list.

Keep playing your lovely good video memory that presents the good picture A in your mind, so you are choosing a happy playlist. Now instruct your mind to give you more and more happy memories to add to it! Your mind will learn what you want and serve you kindly and, most of all, help you heal.

Sometimes, having just lost your adored pet, it can be so overwhelming. Even to the point that you won't go out / visit friends. The 'fear' of seeing another that is similar, or someone simply enjoying time with their pet, will trigger such emotion, that you feel you would not be able to cope. You also do not want to experience yet more emotional pain. This can lead to all sorts of problems such as cutting yourself off from normal life and from those who really can help and support you.

You are in grief and do you know what will trigger these emotions? The feelings which can make you wish you had never gone out? You really do not want to feel like this, do you? Why would you? It will not help you in any shape or form. You are in emotion so instead of beating yourself up, be kind to yourself. Tell your mind the better way to deal with this.

You can instruct at these times to recall the good video memory picture A. Allow it to expand and fill your mind, bringing with it the more positive feelings.

Also, try this process: Take a deep breath and visualise the potential trigger (i.e. seeing another pet or talking about what has happened) and ask your mind, 'What is the best way for me to feel at that time?' The *best* way is going to be *best* for you. Your mind should offer what is good like, for example, 'Calm, peaceful, and enjoy seeing those animals being happy.' Your words maybe different but good all the same, after all, you are instructing your mind to give you the *best* advice. (It will hardly suggest, 'break down in tears and run home.' NO!) Once you have got those words, repeat them to yourself over and over. For example, self instruct 'When I see another dog, I shall remain calm, peaceful, and enjoy seeing them being happy.' You will be putting that instruction and words into your mind to be used at that time. Repeat, repeat and even write them down if you need to.

Imagine, no more fear and hiding away. When someone's sweet animal that tries to give you love and comfort, you will want to accept it and not feel like you shouldn't. After all, so many animals sense our pain and will lovingly try to help you. They get as much out of helping you, as you being nice to them. Embrace it, they are helping you heal. You would have been proud of your own animal trying to help someone who is grieving, would you not?

I will address another point here. Some people feel so guilty as they are missing their animal but their other animal is overly craving attention from them. Their animal is missing their friend but, due to the fact that we are so upset, sometimes we cannot cope with giving total affection at that time. Again, you should not to be hard on yourself – we are human and things are often hard to cope with. (Maybe following some of the techniques / thought processes in this book, a little less so. I do hope so.) As time passes, things get back to normal and your other pet will be as they always were with you. Think of it like this… sometimes when an animal is ill, they do not want you constantly at them, and will turn away / not be their usual self. They can't cope with you as they need peace to get over what is happening to them at that time. It is all emotion, just a different one!

Here also is another healing process that is clever and easy to understand and do. Not only will this help with Pet Grief, but our life's struggles too.

Think of your mind like the computer workings, as I mentioned earlier. We all know how to 'delete' on a computer, so if a memory comes forward and you do not want it, picture sending it straight to the TRASH bin – or in your mind press, DELETE, if you prefer.

Can you remember that I said our minds are so clever that they 'helpfully' like to link things up for you? Great for all the positive things in life when you need to be resourceful as any buried knowledge helps. However, it does the same with sad and unhelpful things.

So, for a minute, think of yourself like a laptop. The screen is your present mind and the keyboard part is where all your memories are stored. (Screen being your conscious and the keyboard area being your sub-conscious.) If you want to organise your mind better, again sit down and get comfortable.

From your mind, think about something that is hurting you and up on your screen (your present thoughts) something relevant will come up. You will see it and then ask for all the files (memories) associated with it too. Every time one pops up, visually send it to TRASH, or in your mind, visually press DELETE. Be tough on your mind and ask it for more, you will be safe doing this as you now know, you can instantly remove it. (Think of it like an email that has a warning about a virus, do not open (therefore acknowledging) but delete straightaway. Repeat and repeat, and often things may flood into your mind you had forgotten about but your 'clever' mind had stored anyway. Send to TRASH / DELETE and when you feel that sense of relief and your brain has 'run out of things' at present, then do the last step…

In your mind, instruct it to empty the TRASH or RECYCLING BIN. Think of it all disappearing into cyber space. If this helps… I use the visual of the thoughts as loads of bits of paper floating out in the sky and the wind taking them further and further away, until they are specks in the distance and no longer able to be seen or return. No longer are they able to cause upset in your computer, which of course is your mind.

I have done this one so many times and really, it does help. It gives room for the more sensible, kinder programs to run and helps me use my mind with less junk, un-useful information in it.

Once again my credit goes to Maureen for these techniques. They truly can be life-changing and take away so much pain that we often believe that we have to keep living with. We don't!

Moving Forward

This is often something many cannot bear to think about. Of course, this is all dependent on what stage of grief you are at – how far through the Grief Curve you have got.

We all may say and think that we may 'let our animal down' if we get another. I have clients who ask me to ask their spirit animal this very question. I can say, hand on heart, animals want you to be happy. They often point out how amazing and loving you were with them and the happiness it brought to you – so why would they not want you to experience that happiness again? And also, giving it to another pet so they can experience it too. Animals know they have had their life, however long, and just want you to be happy.

Let's turn this around. Even if you do not believe in Heaven/Spirit etc. for a moment, just pretend to yourself that you do.

So, you are now the one in Heaven and your pet was your keeper. As you watch, would you want them to live in solitude, not love another, not enjoy sharing time with another person? I bet you have answered your own question! Of course not – you would want them to be happy. So, in reverse?...

Life is precious and we do not know where our ending is!

I smile as I write this as, although I hope helped give you some clarity there, how many times have you heard, or said, 'I had no intention of getting another animal'? Yes, and it happened anyway.

We really are not in charge and, if an animal is to come to you, it will! I am sure some of you are now smiling to yourselves too. Having experienced this when another 'arrived' to bring you such joy, or lessons, as is even sometimes is the case.

In many of my books I have said, 'Whatever animal will come to you, will!' I often wondered why this happened and one day a spirit dog was kind enough to inform me. He told me that we have 'Soul Families' and these families are set out so animals and people are all destined to be part of it. As I write this, I am sure there will be some of you that will have dreamt of an animal, and then that animal arrived! You might be the one nodding! The reason being is that spirit are showing you another member of your Soul Family. So much is pre-destined so, if you want to take a leaf out of my book, (not literally as you may lose the page) I live by the saying, 'What is for you, won't go past you'. This gives me acceptance even if things don't go the way I thought they should have.

When some people lose a pet, they instantly go out and get another puppy/kitten or whatever. I know that people are often very surprised, and sometimes judgmental about this.

That is the healing process that those owners are to have and that new animal will help them. We are all very different in our thoughts. Animals are not naturally judgmental, however should they suffer fear etc. then yes, this can cause them to judge and act out of self- protection.

We as babies and young children started like that too. However, being a human is very complicated and we have many thought processes. We all do things differently and I myself have faults – I am human. Would you think it possible to ever be perfect as a human being? Being human, part of our journey is about mistakes and learning. However, sometimes, it is a good thing to just swop places in your mind with the person you are judging, and you may see a different picture. What happens in our lives makes us who we are. Saying that, you are maybe getting the gist that some things really do not have to stay with us, or affect us. We can tell our minds what to do – they are our own minds and we shall try our best to program to serve us as best possible.

My take on this someone getting a new pet straightaway was because it was supposed to come to them when it did. Remember the Soul Family I explained about? Destiny is, well… destiny!

In readings I have on occasion given the name of an animal that the owner did not know of. Incredibly that animal came into their life – it still amazes me and it was me that told them! (Names really are often difficult to get, but I just pass what I hear and when things like this are validated, it brings me such joy and more proof of the way life is mapped out for us.)

This really makes me smile… I have had the pleasure to do a reading for a lovely couple who are in their senior years. So very kind, but sadly have experienced quite a few cat bereavements over the past few years. On the last spirit reading I did, I gave them the name Billy. They did not know who Billy was. I said to note it as I am being passed the name for some reason and maybe a new boy for them? A while later I got an email letting me know that they had found themselves a new cat. They had gone to a rescue centre and straightaway spotted a girl cat, with the name 'Billie' on her cage! Needless to say, another part of their soul family is living with them.

Here is another from one of my clients…

My reading from my dog Hamish in spirit, mentioned 'Daisy'. I thought maybe somewhere on the dog walking scene we had come across a Daisy, but nothing profound sprung to my mind. About 20 months later, and not really planned, 'Daisy' came into our lives!

She is a rescue dog and now very loved and wanted. I checked my piece of paper from my reading and, Yes! There was the name Daisy written down – She truly was Heaven sent.

Alison – Essex

One bit of information that did make me smile was not a name, but the vision of following a very obvious big backend of a black and white horse! The lady in question was having a spirit reading for her horse. Her horse offered the picture but she said she did not even know a coloured horse. She noted it anyway. A couple of weeks later I received an email to say, a kindly friend had offered to let her ride her horse. They went out with a group of people on their horses and suddenly she realised, she was following right behind an obvious large backend of a black and white horse! Amazing how her horse knew that was going to happen. It brought her great comfort.

Whilst I am here, I hope you don't mind me sharing this very sweet one from a client who had the horse of a lifetime, which was most of his lifetime…

After I lost my beloved horse Wiz, I was absolutely heart-broken. He was my best friend, partner and soul-mate and for 23 years, I was blessed to share his life. During his spirit reading he gave the name Ella. I had no idea who Ella was. Roll on two weeks and a new young horse came onto the yard. When I asked her name, you could have knocked me over with a feather. Ella's new owner had only just found her, and bought her instantly as she really was in poor condition. She is now blooming and it gives me such pleasure to know that Wiz knew she was coming. Perhaps he even helped guide her to our yard to be loved and cared for, like they all are.

Louise – Telford

I hope that really helps you knowing that if they can tell us these things, that so much is set out for us and also, that they do live on in spirit.

As in life, we learn as we go, sometimes the wrong way and sometimes the right. I do believe that mistakes are there for us to learn from and realise that we are human, we *will* make mistakes. We are not perfect, we are not all medically trained and do the best we can with the knowledge we have at the time.

Even when it seems so unfair that your adorable animal has suffered from various conditions and in the end, nothing could save them. Maybe, you learnt of treatments that you did not previously know, and they made a difference.

There are so many alternative medicines and treatments out there and people willing to share their information and experiences. I am not against conventional medicine at all, but having experienced some amazing changes with Homeopathy, Acupuncture, I truly have an open mind. Often conventional and alternative can go hand in hand and whatever can help your pet has to be a good thing. I always suggest to my clients that they do their own research and check out reviews etc. The great thing nowadays is that you can get information from the internet and people like to share their stories. (Talking of reviews – if you think this book can help others, then please write a review. People always read reviews before they buy. So, for a few minutes of your time, your efforts could help ease someone's suffering too. Thank you.) Sometimes we cannot change the outcome but most clouds have silver linings.

Here is another from one of my clients…

My dog Oscar was poorly his entire life and we had to make so many decisions about his care. After his early death, we constantly questioned ourselves — should we have done a) instead of b) etc. I was consumed by guilt, regret and remorse. I know I tried everything and even learnt much about herbal remedies to help him. During his reading, he said that his death and health problems was nobody's fault, it was just the way he was made and it was just his pre-destined time to go. No-one was to blame. He said to use what I had learnt to help others and call it 'Oscar's Remedy'. I realised that through him, and his ailments, I have gained a lot of knowledge to help others. This made a huge impact on me and helped me heal.

Lorraine — Lincoln

*****

In Memory of, and Signs from Spirit

Sally Feb 7th 2005 – Sept 14th 2018

If you are surprised to see the dates for dear Sally here, I am as surprised to be writing this at this time. It is less than a week since she has passed, so I am finishing this book going through the grief process myself. Not only was she so very loved personally, but by so many friends and had a huge following on Facebook too.

I really am trying to use all that I have learnt, and shared with you, to travel this grief journey in the smoothest and strongest way I can. I have got readings booked in and do not want to let anybody down. After all, I am often part of helping someone else's grieving process.

I started this book on 1st September 2018 (Stan's anniversary) as I felt pushed from spirit to do so. The stories that I included from my clients, were given to me via Facebook in the first week too. Little did I know that by the Friday 14th, I would be with my girl for her last breath on Earth.

On that Friday, at three in the morning, I could not sleep. I got up, sat at my computer completing this book. I worked solidly throughout the night. What I did not know was that Sally (who was 50 miles away from me) was being very sick throughout the night. Bob got her to the vets in the morning and she was put on a saline drip. He phoned me on the way and said she really was very, very poorly.

This came as a shock as, in spite of the strokes, she was as bright as a button the day before. The night before, she scoffed her dinner and went to bed as usual. Bob kept me informed and I asked him to phone the vets after a couple of hours instead of waiting until the 3pm as they had suggested. He did that and they informed him that they had done tests. Devastatingly, when they did an ultrasound on her tummy they could see a tumour on her liver or spleen and fluid inside her abdomen too. (Sometimes animals show no symptoms until they have a bleed or suchlike.)

We instantly knew that this was her last day. There was no going back and having suffered such pain from my own liver cancer, there was no way we wanted any intervention. It would have been futile and, at this point in time, she was not in pain and being kept comfortable.

I jumped in the car and drove the fifty miles to be with her. Together, Bob and I went to the vets. When in emotional state, it is so hard to communicate with your own pets, and especially this precious precious girl. As I drove, I did my best and she volunteered, 'I am done'.

We had already decided that if she was going to Heaven, that to be put to sleep in the back of her car would be a fitting place. She adored being in the car. Even if you were just going to the shops, she wanted to come anyway.

Before we arrived at the vets, we had decided that we could carry her out to the car ourselves. We wanted to spend this last bit of quality time with her. I asked them if we could do this but they suggested that we go and sit with her in the kennels instead, which we did. There was no longer the light in her beautiful eyes, although she definitely knew we were both there.

After about 20 minutes, I got the strength to go and repeat my request and said that we wanted to spend quality time with her and that it would not cause her suffering to do so. They listened this time and we carried her out to the car. (I have tried in this book to say that we have rights and so try to be strong so get to do what you want to. After all, they are our pets and we want what gives us, and them, the most peace possible at this exceedingly hard and gut wrenching time. Sometimes your efforts may fall on deaf ears, but at least in your heart, you know you have tried and not just accepted without trying.)

Beautifully, the sun was shining and we laid her comfortably on her blanket in the boot area of the car. We had such precious quality time with her and said all that we could think of. She told me she was not scared and was 'Going to Traverse the Universe! I would never have thought of those words and have never had them said to me. This was her way of validating to me, in the midst of my emotion, that it truly was her telling me. This gave us great peace and knowing that she would be going on a great journey having done her time on Earth.

The vet came out and gave her that last injection. She was gone in seconds – peaceful was an understatement. Our Angel's soul had gone to Heaven and we took her body home.

We had done some practical previous mental planning and she was to have an individual cremation. The pet cremation place was back in a little town very near to where we used to live. It was where I had first set eyes on her at the vets there, and, as they say, the rest is history. The place we went to, we actually used to ride past on our horses, so all very fitting.

Even through her cremation, here is another valid point to share with you, so thank you Sally, once again…

I was so saddened to find out, that often in the veterinary 'profession', pet cremation is also being viewed on the monetary scale and help towards said targets. I will not go into finer details but will say to you... Please, in your planning, decide where *you* would prefer your pet / animal to go. You can ask for details or take the information from websites themselves. When the time comes, contact the pet funeral place *direct*. This way you can inform your vet that you wish to take your animal away with you, or that you have already instructed the pet cremation people to collect for you. This way you have control and your wishes will be met. This will help give you peace knowing the choice and place was yours, not elsewhere for another monetary target to be met.

Please do not get me wrong, some vets are amazing. The vets who looked after Sally for years and on her very last day, were so kind, and honest. It took a simple ultrasound to see her tumours and we were not guided to have an MRI (at huge cost) to see basically the same, which could not be fixed anyway. They respected our wishes to let her go and agreed it was the fairest thing. The peaceful passing is what has helped us through, and I thank them wholeheartedly for everything.

However, many of you will be reading / listening to social media and having had your own experiences, know that this is not always the case. I do not wish to bring doom and gloom but, I hope that should you feel things are not quite as you want, then you have the right, and strength to ask. Remember the chapter, *'Don't be Afraid to Ask or Say.'*

As I write this, I am filled with emotion and thoughts of Sally. If I went back in my life, years ago I would have been inconsolable and have struggled to even do my daily work. I know people have that huge problem of going back to their jobs and trying to function. I am sure many of you have been there.

Even worse, you get the person that says, 'It was just an...' This 'cuts like a knife' however, at this point in time, do some pre-planning – brain instructing.

'If anybody ever says anything like that to me, I will pity them as they have obviously never experienced the depth of love that I have had from an animal.'

Repeat it, or re-read it a few times. It will sink into your sub-conscious and at that point when needed, you will recall it and simply pity them. They will not be allowed to affect your emotions, and if they do, get tapping on your chest and breathe it all out.

That photo and words will probably bring tears to your eyes. It does me, for many reasons.

Having a pet will bless you with the happiest days of your life and one of the worst days too.

Tears of her loss but tears of joy as she is now back with Stan and playing once again. I do not expect all of you reading this book to be spiritual and believe in the afterlife. However, it would be wrong for me not to share some of the amazing signs from Sally the next day. I would like to share them with you. They have brought me such comfort and are helping me through my grief process, I hope that they might also help you too. Before I do the day after, I will share an amazing gentle nudge from spirit that was given a few weeks before her passing and not found until afterwards.

Bob was never one for technology but had recently bought an iPad. He managed to do a few things on it and took a few photos too. The evening that Sally passed, I offered to sort out a screensaver for him, using one of the pictures of her.

I looked at the photo gallery and there were about a dozen pictures and one video. I asked him if he knew what the video was and he said no, as he had just tried it to see how it worked.

I pressed play and to my utter delight it is ten seconds of him videoing Sally sitting happily looking at him. That may not seem unusual at all, but this is the bit that took our breath away. The music playing in the background was from the TV and was, 'Alright Now'. That in itself is amazing and what is more incredible is the band is called FREE! I truly believe that was a sign from above as what would the chances of that be? I know that all animals in spirit are 'alright' and 'free' but what lovely confirmation to be given. When you are spiritual you do notice signs maybe easier than people who are not. However, Sally absolutely went to town to show me some and I will share a few and the photos that I took at the time too...

When we arrived home with her body, we placed her on her comfy bed and to be honest, she just looked like she was sleeping. That was a comfort. I offered to make a coffee, as you do.

Just then, I found myself drawn to the coffee table that was strewn with various magazines and bits of paper. I felt I was being made to look. After a minute, I realised that the bit of paper poking out from underneath a magazine, clearly had the letters on it to spell S A L L Y in big turquoise dotted letters. I pointed this out to Bob and then pulled it out to see what it was. The complete words appeared and read... SAY HELLO!!

Wow, words failed us at that point. The slogan is from EE, the mobile phone people. The advert and posters are everywhere, so every time I see one, instantly I will think of her and from my mind say 'Hello'. What a clever clever girl to organise that one!

After we went to the crematorium, we headed into the small town to pass time so we could collect her ashes later. As we drove in, I spotted a rough wooden board plonked on top of a car. On it was painted roughly, 'Garage Sale', complete with arrow.

I pointed it out to Bob so we turned round and went back as I felt we should go. As we looked past the two people sitting on deck chairs, we were surprised to see very little in the rather small garage. However, I felt we were there for a reason so we stepped in and had a look.

Straightaway I saw on the table, not one, but two small pictures comprised of a white butterfly behind glass. (Anyone who knows me well, will remember I have a passion for butterflies and even do my work in what I call, the 'butterfly house' in my garden.)

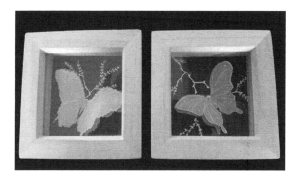

It took our breath away and the man actually gave them to us when we, through our tears, told him the relevance of them.

We drove up to the golf course where we often took her. As we went in, on the right hand side was a massive plastic banner on the grass with the word 'Newlife'. I had no idea what it was for, but I knew it was a lovely sign once again.

We were passing a charity shop which I had no intention of going into and even stated that! (That is so not like me as I love charity shops but this did not seem the time or place.) However, right at the door I felt pushed to go in, so we did. Straight away I was drawn to the back of the shop. Propped up on the floor was a Joseph Farquharson picture of a shepherd with his collie, who is just like Sally. There have been another two from this artist in the house for years as they really are uncanny how alike they are to Sally and Bob.

We collected her ashes in a beautiful wooden casket which was to stay at Bob's house, which was the right thing to do. We then tried to work out where best to place them in the sitting room. I suggested somewhere in front of him whilst he was watching TV. He said he would rather her be on the unit at the back so she could watch over him. We moved a few bits out of the way. However, the casket would not fit back as far as it should. We reached behind and found a picture face down. Incredibly it was one that I had left behind which was of hands holding the world up in the universe. Gosh, she had said about 'Traversing the Universe' and there was the picture to go with it.

A Pet's Love from Heaven

From this body we shall leave, but remember
It is only our body that fails to breathe
Still our souls will float on high
Never leaving us to wonder why
We know our days are given and destiny set
We lived our life and here we are met.
Our lives are special and to be treasured
Love and laughter in equal measure
Whether a quiet one or more 'in-your-face'
Your lives our never ending love did grace.
We ask for no tears or sorrow
You have love and a tomorrow
We watch over you and with a smile
For we will be together again, in a while.
If another animal now needs your special love,
This too can be guided from us above.
We can watch and steer, even sometimes interfere.
We will smile as you say, 'Oh they did that too'
Of course they do, as we listen to you!
You taught us well and showed us much
We still remember your love and touch
I may even have been a bit of a 'monkey'
But perhaps more of an Angel too

This does not matter, for I was sent to YOU!
My living breathing days are over now
But on I shall go and with this I vow,
It is not over, this is just the here and now.
Please learn to laugh and forget any pain
You will smile and be happy again.
As for me, I was a treasure to beholden
Sharing your days and hours truly golden.
I am not crying for my love is still as strong
And I know that I am back where I belong.
One day you will grace us with your presence
Give me kisses and loving effervescence
I sent you my love and thank my lucky stars
All because I was sent to be yours!

Guess who helped me write that? Sally, of course. They really can help to guide us on Earth, so send up your thoughts and you just never know. If this has brought tears to your eyes, and you no longer want to cry… I do hope you know what to do! Look upwards, tap, and breathe.

My hope is that spirit has guided me well and that this book has really helped you. Everyone can do the practical mental planning, believe you me, in time, you will be so glad you did.

Even if you do not go with all that I have written here for you, I hope that some things will really have made you think, and even give a try. The processes have made such a difference to so many and guess what, they are free for you to do! In this world, there is not much you get for free – but your mind is yours, and you can help... YOU!

I hope that I have instilled some strength into your thoughts when you may need to be strong and have a voice for your animals.

We are so blessed to have them and love them. Grief is all part of loving someone – I hope that this book will help you cope with your pet grief, before and after.

We all have so many special moments and love from our animals. So in their honour, we shall try to be happy and concentrate on the wonderful times, after all, they will be reminiscing with us too.

*****

Postscript

On my website you can also find the link to my You-Tube channel. You will see there is a video of me chatting to Fiona's cat, Jezzy, who is 19 at that time and does a wonderful job of letting us know, about quality of life in the typical, straightforward way that animals do. You may find it helpful if you have an animal of senior years.

Thank you so very much to all my wonderful friends, Shirley, Moyra, Maureen and Kathy who have checked this book – your help and opinions are invaluable. If you want to know more about NLP, EFT and other fantastic life-changing skills, here is Maureen's, an Emotional and Behavioural expert. website: www.maureenfearon.co.uk

I also have a monthly Animal Communication column in Chat It's Fate magazine. If you want to be kept informed of what I am getting up to, TV appearances, what my next book is etc. I do send out the occasional newsletter. If you go on to my website and scroll down to the bottom of the first page, you will see a picture of my cat Buddy looking inquisitive and you can sign up from there. I promise, your email address is totally protected and never shared.

Thank you for choosing and reading this book.

Although this was not based on animal communication, if you are interested in what I do and

want to read more, here are the other books that I have written too.

They are all available on Amazon in paperback and Digital. As usual, I have kept my price low as I want people to be able to read, learn and enjoy.

If you don't mind me asking (again!) but, if you can spare a minute to write a review about this book (or any other of mine that you have read) I would be most grateful. It is the public's opinion that helps others make their choice of reading material.

So, if you feel this book would be informative, enjoyable or even enlightening to someone else, a few words would help guide them. You too may also help change their life.

It has been through the kindness, knowledge and help that people have shown to me, that I am in the place where I am today, which is to help people and animals alike.

In life, if we can make a positive difference, even if just a small one, then we are living and helping others in our own unique way.

Darling Sally

Never Ending Love

Jackie Weaver

'The Animal Psychic'

www.animalpsychic.co.uk

www.petgrief.co.uk

Printed in Great Britain
by Amazon